Halloween

by **Trudi Strain Trueit**

Reading Consultant: Nanci R. Vargus, Ed.D.

Marshall Cavendish
Benchmark
New York

Picture Words

 bats

 candy

 ghosts

 jack-o'-lanterns

 masks

 moon

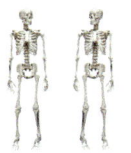 skeletons

 spiders

 witches

The 🌕 is out
on Halloween!

It is time for 🎃🎃🎃.

It is time for .

It is time for 🧙🧙🧙.

It is time for .

It is time for 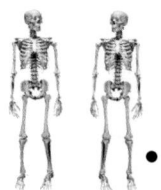.

It is time for 🦇.

It is time for .

It is time for 🎃.
Trick or treat!

Words to Know

Halloween (hal-uh-WEEN)
  a holiday on October 31, celebrated by children in costumes asking for treats

jack-o'-lanterns (JAK-uh-lant-uhrns)
  pumpkins that are carved and lit for Halloween

Find Out More

Books

Heiligman, Deborah. *Celebrate Halloween*. Washington, D.C.: National Geographic Society, 2007.

Mercer, Abbie. *Happy Halloween*. New York: PowerKids Press, 2008

Old, Wendie C. *The Halloween Book of Facts and Fun*. Morton Grove, IL: A. Whitman, 2007.

Websites

Making Friends.Com: Halloween Crafts
www.makingfriends.com/halloween.htm
PBS Kids: Halloween Activities
http://pbskids.org/halloween
United Nations Children's Fund: Trick-or-Treat for UNICEF
http://youth.unicefusa.org/trickortreat

About the Author
Trudi Strain Trueit loved coming up with weird Halloween costumes when she was a kid. (She went trick-or-treating one year as cotton candy.) She is the author of more than fifty fiction and nonfiction books for children, including *Thanksgiving* and *Valentine's Day* in the Benchmark Rebus Holiday Fun series. Visit her website at **www.truditrueit.com**.

About the Reading Consultant
Nanci R. Vargus, Ed.D., wants all children to enjoy reading. She used to teach first grade. Now she works at the University of Indianapolis. Nanci helps young people become teachers. She loves sewing Halloween costumes. Of the fifty she has made for her daughters and grandchildren, her favorite was baby Christopher's leopard seal costume.

Copyright © 2011 Marshall Cavendish Corporation

Published by Marshall Cavendish Benchmark
An imprint of Marshall Cavendish Corporation

All rights reserved.

No part of this publication may be reproduced, stored in a retrieval system or transmitted, in any form or by any means, electronic, mechanical, photocopying, recording, or otherwise, without the prior permission of the copyright owner. Request for permission should be addressed to the Publisher, Marshall Cavendish Corporation, 99 White Plains Road, Tarrytown, NY 10591. Tel: (914) 332-8888, fax: (914) 332-1888.

Website: www.marshallcavendish.us

This publication represents the opinions and views of the author based on Trudi Strain Trueit's personal experience, knowledge, and research. The information in this book serves as a general guide only. The author and publisher have used their best efforts in preparing this book and disclaim liability rising directly and indirectly from the use and application of this book.

Other Marshall Cavendish Offices:
Marshall Cavendish International (Asia) Private Limited, 1 New Industrial Road, Singapore 536196 • Marshall Cavendish International (Thailand) Co Ltd. 253 Asoke, 12th Flr, Sukhumvit 21 Road, Klongtoey Nua, Wattana, Bangkok 10110, Thailand • Marshall Cavendish (Malaysia) Sdn Bhd, Times Subang, Lot 46, Subang Hi-Tech Industrial Park, Batu Tiga, 40000 Shah Alam, Selangor Darul Ehsan, Malaysia

Marshall Cavendish is a trademark of Times Publishing Limited

All websites were available and accurate when this book was sent to press.

Library of Congress Cataloging-in-Publication Data
Trueit, Trudi Strain.
Halloween / Trudi Strain Trueit.
    p. cm. — (Benchmark rebus. Holiday fun)
Includes bibliographical references.
Summary: "A simple introduction to Halloween using rebuses"—Provided by publisher.
ISBN 978-0-7614-4886-0
1. Halloween—Juvenile literature. 2. Rebuses—Juvenile literature. I. Title.
GT4965.T78 2009
394.2646—dc22
2009019069

Editor: Christina Gardeski
Publisher: Michelle Bisson
Art Director: Anahid Hamparian
Series Designer: Virginia Pope

Photo research by Connie Gardner
Cover photo by Mel Yates/*Getty Images*
The photographs in this book are used by permission and through the courtesy of:
SuperStock: p. 5 Prisma; p. 9 age fotostock. *Getty Images*: p. 2 Dorling Kindersley, bats, candy; Andy Crawford, ghosts; Ferguson and Katzman, jack-o'-lanterns; CSA Platock, masks; p. 3 Vito Palmisano, moon; Brand X Pictures, skeletons; Andy Crawford, spiders; Paul and Lindamarie, witches; p. 7 Lawrence Lawry; p. 11 Rachel Weill; p. 15 George Doyle; p. 17 Evan Sklar. *Alamy*: p. 13 Sebastien Baussais; p. 19 Spike Mafford. *Corbis*: p. 21 Ariel Skelley.

Printed in Malaysia (T)
1 3 5 6 4 2